INNER FITNESS
for Celebrating Your Life

*Journal through your journey
and expand into yourself*

Rebecca Evans

an **INSIDEOUT** Journal Series

Copyright 2008 by Inner Element,
Rebecca Evans & InsideOut Publishing

All rights reserved. This journal, or parts thereof, may not be reproduced in any form without prior written permission.

Inner Fitness: Celebrating Your Life Journal Series
1st Edition

ISBN 13: 978-0-9815802-2-7

Disclaimer

The services and products offered are exclusively owned by Inner Element, LLC, all rights reserved. The author(s) of these programs do not dispense medical advice or prescribe the use of any technique as a form of treatment for physical or medical problems without the advice of a physician, either directly or indirectly. The author(s) and publisher assume no responsibilities for your actions.

InsideOut Publishing is subsidiary of Inner Element. LLC.

This journal is dedicated to the Women's Fitness Celebration, especially Lorene Oates and Anne Audain, who have brought women together, year after year, of every age, ability, shape and size, simply to celebrate women! We are not our bodies, we are so much more than our physical selves, yet we rarely take a moment to embrace the place we are in and the lives we are living. Anne and Lorene have helped women all over the world discover their potential and find their significance. They have offered encouragement when there was little light. They have offered healing where there was suffering. They have shared their lives, experiences and wisdom with abundance. I not only appreciate these ladies, I admire their bravery. Because of many women around the world just like them, we are able to heal and love ourselves again.

Learning to celebrate life is one of the best lessons a person needs to learn.
~ Joan Chittister

Writing a journal means that facing your ocean, you are afraid to swim across it, so you attempt to drink it drop by drop.
~ George Sand

The publication and distribution of this book would not have been possible without the support and assistance of the following individuals:

Anne Audain	Judy Fuller
Laurie Brede	Vonda Richards
Fritz Eymann	Dennis Weigt

Our sincere thanks to each of them!

Idaho Women's Health Fitness & Education Celebration, Inc.

FOREWORD

It is with great pleasure that I write the foreword for Rebecca's book/journal. I support her passion and dedication in empowering women to embrace their own lives in a positive light. She sincerely embodies the mission of the Celebration; our actions and reactions are derived from our self-esteem, self-respect, and sense of well-being.

I frequently title my speeches *Why Walk When You Can Fly?* I firmly believe we can do anything we set our minds to, but only with patience, perseverance and a positive attitude. I have had an amazing life, certainly full of ups and downs, but out of every tough challenge a wonderful new world has opened up to me and I was able to fully embrace each experiences as an opportunity.

I am often asked, "How did you do it?" Rebecca's company Inner Element offers a great response to this question. I feel that I have always been able to draw on an inner strength, to trust my instincts and intuition even when other forces were working against me. Listening to yourself in this way is not easy. It requires self-honesty and personal responsibility. It has required me to be completely accountable for my life, assigning no blame and having no regrets.

I was adopted at birth and born with bone deformities of both feet. After reconstructive surgery at age 13, I discovered I could run better than I could walk. One year later, I joined a running club and the rest is history. Since that time, I have achieved my goals of qualifying for five Olympic Games, winning a gold medal in the Commonwealth Games and holding the world record in the 5,000 meters.

In other words, I wanted to soar and I did. Running has been my catalyst, my platform in life to help me make a difference in the world. But I also needed the other important components we all require to move forward and succeed—to be loved, nurtured, encouraged, mentored and coached. My mother has the most positive attitude of anyone I know. "No use crying over spilled milk" is the motto she lived by. Too often we wallow in self-pity, self doubt, and look at life as a glass half empty instead of half full.

Along the way, I have encountered people who were certainly not on my side. It is tough to acknowledge to yourself that not everyone is happy for you or wishes that you will succeed. Becoming independent of this negativity is essential. Only then can you live a successful life. And remember, it is not selfish to focus on yourself. The better you are as a human being, the better the world around you will become.

So all of this brings me to Rebecca's journal. I kept journals throughout my 22-year sporting career. Journaling allowed me to note my training regimen and racing results and to recall my goals of daily discipline and good health. My journals were extremely valuable to me as records, and I had to go back and read them a lot; they kept me on course. Sometimes they reminded me I was doing just fine. When you have success, there is a temptation to want to "do more—even more." My journals helped me stay grounded and understand that I had a good formula, that drastic change was unnecessary.

I have been retired for 15 years, and though I no longer journal, I use my daily runs as a form of meditation, a time for reflection and conversation with myself. It often feels like I solve the world's problems while out on those runs. I practice my speeches and relieve myself of any stress I may be feeling. This is the time that I smell the flowers around me, that I celebrate my life.

Writing down your thoughts and feelings in a journal can have all the same effects.

As you go forward on your own journey, in your own way, I would like to leave you with a simple goal: Live simply. Love generously. Care deeply. Speak kindly. Take care of you and become all that you can be!

~ Annie Audain, Olympian and Founder,
St. Luke's Women's Fitness Celebration

INTRODUCTION

This journal—third in my Inner Fitness series—is the one that I feel most inspired about. For ten years I have participated in the St. Luke's Women's Fitness Celebration. I first performed on stage as an athlete, later as a Fitness Professional, then as a speaker, and now as a writer. This Celebration has seen me through many phases in my life: singlehood, career development, pregnancies, and more change and transformation than I can say. The experience of this event is something that I've longed to capture in words. I feel that I have come close to accomplishing such a tall order in this journal.

At the Celebration, women of all abilities, backgrounds and ages come together. They meet for three days and celebrate each other, wherever they may be in their journey in life. This uniting of women is, to me, the essence of the Celebration.

I've watched in awe and from a distance as Annie Audain was inducted into the 2008 Hall of Champions from Running USA—an honor that this stunningly accomplished Olympic athlete greatly deserved. She has given so much of herself for the greater good of others through the Celebration, and thus has given so much to women and girls.

Lorene Oates has walked through this event year after year, encouraging all the women involved. All the while she has been climbing her own mountain, battling a weight and body-image issue with so much grace. This year, I've also watched her overcome, remove walls and finally, summit.

This is a good year for each of us to capture success. After all, there is never any better time than this moment, right now. It is so easy for women to take life casually, without much thought, simply going through the motions, for we are so busy in the care of others. My hope is that this journal helps you slow down and embrace yourself, enjoy the place you are currently in, and dream your dreams of tomorrow. I pray this journal inspires you to celebrate being a woman, the individual you were created to be.

As I have shared in past journals, the transformative power of writing, of journaling, has changed my life. Writing has offered me perspective, valuable insight into my own mind, healing, recovery, transcendence, and so much more. I want to share all of this with you.

Writing does not always need to explore the negative. This year, explore your life with great enthusiasm. Journal as though each moment is something to celebrate, something that offers you opportunity for the future. So, as you write, instead of hanging your head in great burden, lift your head high and explore everything that inspires you, all of the dreams and joys that you may have ignored over the years. The more we can celebrate ourselves, the more likely we will fulfill our life's purpose. I created this journal, the entire series, as an act of human encouragement for other women who bravely seek to understand their own minds and hearts.

Along my own journey I have often forgotten to celebrate. Now I recognize how indispensable is the life-bringing act of celebration. The pages of this book await your pen. Through journaling, you will bring the authentic you back to the essence of life.

All of the journals are designed for you to "recycle" throughout your life, year after year. There is not just one year attached to any of them, and you may begin during any calendar month. I journal as a form of writing practice for ten minutes each day. You may explore this process in your own way, on your own time.

Now, go and celebrate you, from the inside out. Bring out the authentic woman in you, if she has been hidden inside of you or neglected, and greet her with love. But most importantly, when you find her, share her with the world.

~ Rebecca Evans

Creating a Workshop Within
Using Inner Element's Workbook/Journals Series

Inner Element combines art, movement, fitness, nutrition, and education to bring self-development to the total person. By discovering our true talents, by establishing clear life goals, by cultivating self-appreciation, we learn to thrive in today's chaotic environment.

At our core we are all made of the same elements. As human beings we have similar desires, the need to feel appreciated, to experience self-worth and a sense of purpose and well-being. Inner Element programs and products help us to examine our core, to create awareness and balance at the very center of our authentic self. Inner Element's objective is to help all live authentic lives.

I have structured this program so that you can succeed anywhere, anyhow. Regardless of your location or schedule, using an Inner Element Workbook or Journal will enable you to create a workshop from within. Inner Element's Inside Out series was developed with key thoughts and acronyms that are catchy and easy to remember. This method will help you remember throughout the day what you have studied.

I encourage you to keep your journals and purchase new ones each year. Re-do the tasks and measure your success along the way. You will see your progress in comparing one journal to another as you grow, transform and become more of you.

As a symbol of your commitment to this journey, please fill in the blanks on the following contract and sign and date the bottom:

Personal Journey Contract

I deserve to have the best life I can dream of—and possibly one that is even better than my dreams. Before I can achieve this life I must commit to being the best that I can be, from the inside out. I am fully committed to the process of this program for _____ weeks (enter the number of weeks or a deadline by which to complete this workbook).

I know all change starts from within, and I am willing to look within and honestly review my heart in order to benefit from the work. I will follow through on all homework assignments and worksheets.

Should I commence this process with others, in either a formal or informal setting, I will honor and respect my peers within this group and keep their personal information confidential..

Sign:_____

Date:_____

Disclaimer

You have permission to fail. You also have permission to quit, have incomplete pages, do the work poorly, not completely finish a task and/or get less than half-way done. With this permission comes a free pass to NOT FEEL GUILTY should any of the above occur.

THIS IS A JOURNEY.

It takes many small steps of failure to finally arrive, to become successful or to finish a project. Look at any incomplete movement in your life as one small step closer to achievement.

I give myself permission to FAIL

Sign:_____

Date:_____

HOW TO USE THIS JOURNAL

Your Way! You may randomly select exercises, worksheets, and months. The only requirement is that you find your own way to complete the process. You are free to find your own path toward self-discovery, searching the journal for what really interests you now, or go through the process month by month. You'll know what works best for you. Either way, your task now is to uncover (or rediscover) deeper meaning in your life.

JANUARY

Celebrate Your Body

January
Celebrate Your Body

The month of renegotiations, January offers us the opportunity to change. When we think of changing ourselves, we usually think of our outer selves, our bodies. But we can lose this exclusively surface attitude toward ourselves—even if we know we have some work to do in the gym. This January, love the body you have been given, and love everything inside of it. Don't forget that you have a heart, soul, and personality.

The first step toward loving yourself inside and out is to accept your body. Let your body be your friend. Appreciate all that your body does for you, day in and day out.

Look at your body as if you were greeting a dear old friend. After all, most of us are able to look at our closest friends with love and forgiveness, excited simply to be in our friend's presence. Just imagine the peace you will know when you change your attitude about your body. Remember, your best friend this year is the physical you! Make this an opportunity to renegotiate your opinion about your body. Reject your need for "perfection"—whatever perfection means!

Now is the time to embrace the body that has carried you through everything—through all of your pain, heartache, laughter, fond memories. You don't have to create a new image; simply allow yourself to accept the amazing machine you already are. Be healthy, but do what is healthy for your body type. Don't worry about the images that women are besieged with on a daily basis. There are so many ways to achieve beauty. When we think about this issue with sanity, we see it's better to be a healthy heavy-set woman than an unhealthy skinny woman. So love yourself the way you are.

Take this time to discover your body's greatest gifts. Begin with a blank page and write all of your best physical traits. Then write down all of your unique qualities. Ask a close friend to name a few of your best attributes, and then write their opinions, too.

- Write "I love my thighs" on your mirror in dry erase marker.
- Write "Freckles are my Friends" on your compact.
- Turn a "liability" into a definite asset. Learn to love the physical, beautiful you.

Celebrate Your Body

You are searching the world for treasure,
but the real treasure is yourself.
– Rumi

Celebrate Your Body

What the caterpillar calls the end of the world,
the master calls a butterfly.
— Richard Bach

Celebrate Your Body

It takes courage to grow up and turn out to be who you really are.
— e.e. cummings

Celebrate Your Body

The most terrifying thing is to accept oneself completely.
— Carl Jung

Celebrate Your Body

Make the most of yourself, for that is all there is of you.
– Ralph Waldo Emerson

Celebrate Your Body

If I had one gift that I could give you, my friend, it would be the ability to see yourself as others see you, because only then would you know how extremely special you are.

– B.A. Billingsly

Celebrate Your Body

If you cannot be a poet, be the poem.
— David Carradine

Celebrate Your Body

A man cannot be comfortable without his own approval.
– Ralph Waldo Emerson

Celebrate Your Body

Celebrate what you want to see more of.
– Thomas J. Peters

Celebrate Your Body

You cannot consistently perform in a manner inconsistent
with the way you see yourself.
– Zig Ziglar

FEBRUARY

Celebrate Your Mind

February
Celebrate Your Mind

February is the month of connection, a month filled with raw emotion and love. Take time this month to connect to your mind and heart. Pay close attention to the things you think and feel. What really matters to you? How do you see nightfall? What details stand out? Are you fearful of the approaching darkness, or do you have a sense of magic and mystery? If you're fearful—and we are all afraid of something—often it's simply a matter of deciding to change your perspective. It sounds easy, and it often is.

Most of us see the world with the vision we were given as children. Each of us feels that the world is a basically good place or a basically bad place. The good news is, we can change how we feel about ourselves and the world. We are never stuck going around and around in circles, in the same old groove. If it's time for you to swerve out of a bad groove, rest easy. You can do it.

Your mind and heart are two things that no one can take from you, and only you hold the power to change them. Moreover, to change your mind and heart is to change your world. You hold the key to your future, and with a simple change in perspective you can unlock any number of locks.

How do you want to see the world? What do you choose to remember?

Writing is an ancient art that does more than simply capture your thoughts. Instead, through the powerful alchemy of the process, writing transforms the way you think and feel about yourself and the world. Writing changes the nature of thought. When we write, we think more deeply, and we go deeper into ourselves, emerging after a writing session transformed—well, that's on a good day, of course.

So explore what empowers you, what you find beautiful, and what you love. Write down the reflections and wonders of your mind, and chart the changing you as she glides across each page.

Write your thoughts about birth, life, death, the afterlife, and all that comes between.

Take time to exercise and stimulate your mind with puzzles, questions, theories, and develop an insatiable hunger for learning new things.

Celebrate Your Mind

A thought is an idea in transit.
— Pythagoras

Celebrate Your Mind

Everything's in the mind. That's where it all starts.
— Mae West

Celebrate Your Mind

Memory is more indelible than ink.
— Anita Loos

Celebrate Your Mind

> The problem with popular thinking is it doesn't require you to think at all.
> – Kevin Myers

Celebrate Your Mind

The ability to concentrate for a considerable time is essential to difficult achievement.
– Bertrand Russell

Celebrate Your Mind

A conclusion is a place where you get tired of thinking.
– Edward DeBono

Celebrate Your Mind

Learning to write is learning to think. You don't know anything clearly unless you can state it in writing.
— S. I. Hayakawa

Celebrate Your Mind

You are today where your thoughts have brought you.
You will be tomorrow where your thoughts take you.
—James Allen

Celebrate Your Mind

Nothing is impossible, unless you think it is.
– Paramahansa Yogananda

Celebrate Your Mind

What we are today comes from our thoughts of yesterday,
and our present thoughts build our life of tomorrow.
Our Life is the creation of our mind.
– Buddha

MARCH

Celebrate Your Spirit

March
Celebrate Your Spirit

Do you ever wonder why you are here? The spirit inside of you, your soul, began a journey without your knowledge, to discover and recover fulfillment. Your spirit is seeking your mission in life.

Celebrate the force inside of you that shouts from time to time and tells you, wake up. This is your spirit, the deepest essence of you, which knows things about you that you can only glimpse. We can develop the ability to listen to our spirit through prayer or meditation or simply by remaining very still and listening.

Celebrate the hunger to make a difference, leave a legacy, stand up for something, and go out and do it. This is your spirit.

Celebrate the empty ache that needs to be filled with unconditional love. This is your spirit.

Celebrate the playful child who is awestruck by a moon in the sky in the middle of the day and all of life's other miracles. This is your spirit.

Embrace your spirit, the soul housed within your beautiful body. This spirit is here on a magical, holy mission that only you are able to accomplish. You cannot discover what your mission is without acknowledging your spirit.

Celebrate Your Spirit

Stop the flow of your words. Open the window of your heart
and let the spirit speak.
— Rumi

Celebrate Your Spirit

When the heart grieves over what it has lost,
the spirit rejoices over what it has left.
– Sufi epigram

Celebrate Your Spirit

I myself do nothing. The Holy Spirit accomplishes all through me.
— William Blake

Celebrate Your Spirit

What lies behind us and what lies before us are tiny matters,
compared to what lies within us.
– Ralph Waldo Emerson

Celebrate Your Spirit

Like an ability or a muscle, hearing your inner wisdom is strengthened by doing it.
– Robbie Gass

Celebrate Your Spirit

I believe that in our constant search for security, we can never gain any peace of mind until we secure our own soul.
– Margaret Chase Smith

Celebrate Your Spirit

Each time a man stands up for an ideal, or acts to improve the lot
of others, or strikes out against injustice, he sends forth
a tiny ripple of hope.
— Robert F. Kennedy

Celebrate Your Spirit

All journeys have secret destinations of which the traveler is unaware.
– Martin Buber

Celebrate Your Spirit

You give your power away when you make someone or something outside of you more important than what is inside of you.
— source unknown

Celebrate Your Spirit

Dwell as near as possible to the channel in which your life flows.
— Henry David Thoreau

APRIL

Celebrate Your Age

April
Celebrate Your Age

Age is not the years we have lived, but the life of experiences we have earned. Therefore we each have different ages inside of us, based on our various journeys—our education, our life experiences, our culture, our successes, our weaknesses. We can be many things at once, grandmothers, Divas, and playful little girls, embracing a new "age" for each day.

Take time this month to recognize the ages you are each day. Maybe your eyes are older than you are; maybe they have seen more pain and anguish than most. Maybe your shoulders are feeling old, carrying the steady weight of bleak moments and sick children.

We all go through difficult and trying periods. The first step toward healing is acknowledging that we really do feel the way we do.

Maybe you are as brilliant as anyone with a PhD when it comes to crunching numbers, but are still in pre-school when it comes to sharing and taking turns.

We need to be honest about our weaknesses. Believe me, we all have them. List your abilities, strengths, and weaknesses, and assign them each an appropriate "age."

If you have the attitude and wonderment of an eager young student, you will stay young in age. Let's remember that we are only groping at the hem of human understanding. It really is humbling how much we all have to learn. As new information and ideas open for you, relax. The more we learn, the more we discover how little we know. Resolve to feel excited when you discover ideas that you know nothing about. When you marvel at the vastness of it all, you discover that you feel very small – or simply very young.

Keep in mind that, in our generation, age 40 is the new 20. You are as young as you believe yourself to be.

Celebrate Your Age

Whether it is the best of times or the worst of times,
it's the only time we've got.
— Art Buchwald

Celebrate Your Age

Old age is not a disease – it is strength and survivorship, triumph over all kindsof vicissitudes and disappointments, trials and illnesses.
– Maggie Kuhn

Celebrate Your Age

*To everything there is a season, and a time
to every purpose under the heaven.*
— Ecclesiastes 3:1

Celebrate Your Age

The best age is the age you are.
— Maggie Kuhn

Celebrate Your Age

Wherever you are is your entry point.
— Kabir

Celebrate Your Age

How far you go in life depends on you being tender with the young, compassionate with the aged, sympathetic with the striving, and tolerant of the weak and the strong. Because someday in life you will have been all of these.
– George Washington Carver

Celebrate Your Age

Do something outrageous every day.
— Maggie Kuhn

Celebrate Your Age

The error of youth is to believe that intelligence is a substitute for experience, while the error of age is to believe that experience is a substitute for intelligence.
— Lyman Bryson

Celebrate Your Age

Age is important no less than youth itself,
though in another dress. And as evening twilight fades away,
the sky is filled with stars invisible by day.
— Henry Wadsworth Longfellow

Celebrate Your Age

You are never too old to set another goal or to dream a new dream.
— C. S. Lewis

MAY

Celebrate Your Ambitions

May
Celebrate Your Ambitions

As we age, many of us begin to suppress our ambitions; we use rationalizations and social pressure to forget who and what we had once wanted to become. After awhile, after too much compromise and capitulation, we can no longer decipher what our hearts are trying to tell us. By this time, we have turned off our connection to our souls. When we constantly seek others' advice and opinions, while negating and denying our true feelings, we become confused and cluttered.

We came into this world knowing the journey held in our hearts. We could feel the right path. Most of us lose sight of our real desires along the way.

But we can begin, at any age, to celebrate and pursue our soul's ambitions and to develop the strength required to carry out the commands of our hearts.

Spend time this month reviewing your lifelong goals, your ambitions. Ask yourself what you used to want to become. Have you accomplish this? Why or why not?

What led you down the path you are on? Where do you want to grow from here?

Honoring your ambitions will keep you on your soul's journey, accomplishing part of the great divine plan you were designed to complete during your mission here. Tune in to your heart, and think large again. Embrace all that you are yet to become.

Celebrate Your Ambitions

Each of us must work for our own improvement.
— Marie Curie

Celebrate Your Ambitions

Character cannot be developed in ease and quiet. Only through experience of trial and suffering can the soul be strengthened, vision cleared, ambition inspired, and success achieved.
– Helen Keller

Celebrate Your Ambitions

Vision without action is merely a dream. Action without vision just passes the time. Vision with action can change the world.
– Joel A. Barker

Celebrate Your Ambitions

Nothing limits achievement like small thinking; nothing expands possibilities like unleashed thinking.
— William Arthur Ward

Celebrate Your Ambitions

Consult not your fears but your hopes and your dreams. Think not about your frustrations, but about your unfulfilled potential. Concern yourself not with what you tried and failed, but with what it is still possible for you to do.
— Pope John XXIII

Celebrate Your Ambitions

Lord, grant that I may always desire more than I accomplish.
– Michaelangelo

Celebrate Your Ambitions

The tragedy of life doesn't lie in not reaching your goal.
The tragedy lies in having no goal to reach.
– Benjamin Mays

Celebrate Your Ambitions

If you want to be happy, set a goal that commands your thoughts, liberates your energy, and inspires your hopes.
– Andrew Carnegie

Celebrate Your Ambitions

The motto 'Always Dream' has served as my personal inspiration for many years. It is my constant reminder to dream big, never lose sight of my goals, and strive to become a better person.
— Kristi Yamaguchi

Celebrate Your Ambitions

Everyone has talent. What is rare is the courage to follow the talent to the dark place where it leads.
— Erica Jong

JUNE

Celebrate Your Dreams

June

Celebrate Your Dreams

When we are awake in our lives, dreams are part of our reality. They offer us another perspective, a different angle on life. When we finally allow our mind to settle, to be still, away from the flow of constant information, the ideas beneath the surface rise to the top, and we can look to our dreams to see what it is that we truly want.

Dreams give us an opportunity to interpret the shapes and patterns of our subconscious selves. What is it that the spirit, veiled and illusive, is trying to say? Let your dream speak to you.

Write down your dreams. Write the dreams you have while you sleep, but include your waking dreams as well.

You, of course, are part of your dream, the waking dream and the sleeping one. There is a piece of you in every detail. With this insight, journal these pieces of yourself. Separate your dream into snippets and unveil the hidden message your underlying consciousness is trying to share with you. Wake up and dream!

Celebrate Your Dreams

We dream into our knowledge with our whole bodies.
— Natalie Goldberg

Celebrate Your Dreams

One has the right to paint one's dreams.
~ Jean-Jacques Rousseau

Celebrate Your Dreams

The more you can dream, the more you can do.
– Michael Korda

Celebrate Your Dreams

Each of us has an inner dream that we can unfold if we will just have the courage to admit what it is. And the faith to trust our own admission.
— Julia Cameron

Celebrate Your Dreams

Nothing happens unless first a dream.
— Carl Sandburg

Celebrate Your Dreams

Hope is a waking dream.
— Aristotle

Celebrate Your Dreams

I have spread my dreams under your feet, tread softly,
because you tread on my dreams.
– William Butler Yeats

Celebrate Your Dreams

The future belongs to those who believe in the beauty
of their dreams.
– Eleanor Roosevelt

Celebrate Your Dreams

Dreams are the touchstones of our character.
– Henry David Thoreau

Celebrate Your Dreams

God gives us dreams a size too big so that we can grow into them.
— Unknown

JULY

Celebrate Your Footprints

July
Celebrate Your Footprints

The paths we are on often reveal that we have taken a detour. Perhaps we are on a random journey through our lives, operating on automatic pilot, going with the flow, doing what everybody else is doing, trying to achieve what society wants us to achieve. And it's okay to get lost from time to time. It's a learning experience. Each event in our lives presents an opportunity, a chance to learn some skill we will need somewhere in our future. We are indeed living our lives in training.

Your path, each step, is taking you on a course that is preparing you for the next great adventure. Glance behind you as if you can see your own footprints on a sandy beach. What are the milestones of your life? Don't forget your accomplishments.

Draw footprints and write in each one the lessons you have learned, experiences gained, or moments embraced—all the stuff of life that offers meaning and value to you at the end of your day.

You alone have traveled this journey. No one can walk in your place. Celebrate each step on your path, even the faulty ones, because, of course, you are only halfway there.

Celebrate Your Footprints

A journey of a thousand miles begins with one step.
— Lao Tzu

Celebrate Your Footprints

We have to believe that every person counts, counts as
a creative force that can move mountains.
– May Sarton

Celebrate Your Footprints

You need to claim the events of your life to make yourself yours.
When you truly possess all you have been and done,
which may take some time, you are fierce with reality.
— Florida Scott-Maxwell

Celebrate Your Footprints

Every day you may make progress. Every step may be fruitful.
Yet there will stretch out before you an ever-lengthening,
ever-ascending, ever-improving path. You know you will never
get to the end of the journey. But this, so far from discouraging,
only adds to the joy and glory of the climb.
– Sir Winston Churchill

Celebrate Your Footprints

You will find as you look back upon your life that the moments
when you have truly lived are the moments when you have
done things in the spirit of love.
— Henry Drummond

Celebrate Your Footprints

Ten perdu, jhamai se recobro. (Time lost can never be regained.)
— A medieval Occitan proverb

Celebrate Your Footprints

My yesterdays walk with me. They keep step,
they are gray faces that peer over my shoulder.
~ William Golding

Celebrate Your Footprints

You cannot change your destination overnight,
but you can change your direction overnight.
— Jim Rohn

Celebrate Your Footprints

The end is nothing; the road is all.
— Willa Cather

Celebrate Your Footprints

When you get to the top of the mountain, your first inclination
is not to jump for joy, but to look around.
– James Carville

AUGUST

Celebrate Your Strengths

August
Celebrate Your Strengths

There is a blueprint within each one of us. We were specially designed, made for a purpose, and part of this design includes a list of things we are good at. Some of these talents may come to us with great ease, others may take hard work and focus, and still other skills may be "under construction." Simply put, some strengths take time to develop.

Sometimes our strengths can hinder us. We may be easy-going in nature, for example, but if we are too nice, to the point where we are taken advantage of, our nature can hinder us in life, leaving us feeling resentful.

For the month of August, list your strengths. List the things you are drawn to, good at, or in the process of developing. Next to your list, write down how these strengths serve you (and others) and how they possibly hold you back.

Your strengths are part of your lessons in life. They exist to teach you appropriate use and care of your gifts.

Celebrate Your Strengths

We are all gifted. That is our inheritance.
— Ethel Waters

Celebrate Your Strengths

Do not wait; the time will never be 'just right'. Start where you stand, and work with whatever tools you may have at your command, and better tools will be found as you go along.

– Napoleon Hill

Celebrate Your Strengths

We must believe that we are gifted for something,
and that this thing, at whatever cost, must be attained.
– Marie Curi

Celebrate Your Strengths

Whether we know it or not, each of us carries our own unique slogan,
a custom-made catchphrase that resonates thoughout our lives
– Marlo Thomas

Celebrate Your Strengths

Meditate. Live purely. Be quiet. Do your work with mastery.
Like the moon, come out from behind the clouds. Shine!
– Buddha

Celebrate Your Strengths

When I dare to be powerful, to use my strength in the service of my vision, then it becomes less and less important whether I am afraid.
– Audre Lorde

Celebrate Your Strengths

Nature never repeats herself, and the possibilities of
one human soul will never be found in another.
– Elizabeth Cady Stanton

Celebrate Your Strengths

Each person's work is always a portrait of himself.
– Samuel Johnson

Celebrate Your Strengths

Be so strong that nothing can disturb your peace of mind.
— Christian Larson

Celebrate Your Strengths

Share our similarities, celebrate our differences.
— M. Scott Peck

SEPTEMBER

Celebrate Your Seasons

September

Celebrate Your Seasons

We do not live life in one long stream; we negotiate life in phases. We grow incrementally as we proceed from infant to child. We learn as we change from a child to a teen, and again into an adult. First we are daughters and sisters, then wives and mothers, and finally grandmothers, each new role hastening startling change.

You don't need to have given birth to experience these phases. As a woman, you are indeed a daughter, sister, wife and mother to someone in your life. We often nurture and mother our friends, bosses or spouses. We are full of cherished wisdom, hovering like a grandmother, "feeding" a project, our community, our acquaintances and peers.

Our seasons are graceful times of rebirth and growth.

As summer turns to fall, as leaves darken and slip from trees, write about your phase in life, the place you currently occupy. Take time to reflect on the place you have recently left.

Discover all that you will cherish about your current season. What does this time offer you? What do you want to offer the world at this time?

Celebrate Your Seasons

When the winds of change blow, some people build walls
and others build windmills.
– Chinese Proverb

Celebrate Your Seasons

It takes a lot of courage to release the familiar
and seemingly secure, to embrace the new.
– Alan Cohen

Celebrate Your Seasons

The unexamined life is not worth living.
— Socrates

Celebrate Your Seasons

Our life's journey is an ever-unfolding work of art that tells the story of where we have been and with whom we have traveled.
– Iyanla Van Zant

Celebrate Your Seasons

There must be a goal at every stage of life.
— Maggie Kuhn

Celebrate Your Seasons

You can become blind by seeing each day as a similar one.
Each day is a different one; each day brings a miracle of it own.
It's just a matter of paying attention to this miracle.
– Paulo Coelho

Celebrate Your Seasons

I don't want to get to the end of my life and find that I lived just the length of it. I want to have lived the width of it as well.
– Source unknown

Celebrate Your Seasons

Good company in a journey makes the way seem shorter.
— Izaak Walton

Celebrate Your Seasons

You must begin to see yourself as becoming the person
you want to be.
– David Viscott

Celebrate Your Seasons

It is good to have an end to journey towards;
but it is the journey that matters in the end.
– Ursula K. Le Guin

OCTOBER

Celebrate a Pause

October

Celebrate a Pause

We have become enormously busy in our hi-tech world, which bombards us with information and tempts us with instant gratification. We are so busy that we are never still, never quiet and restful enough to listen to our own hearts. We are disconnected from the flow of life, from ourselves.

Years ago, when the telephone was introduced in households, many people disliked the concept of talking to someone without seeing them. I doubt most people then anticipated the explosion of technology that today pollutes our culture. With our faces bowed to screens, cell phones, "blackberries," we no longer see nor hear one another.

Fall transforms summer to winter, and we often retreat to the warm comfort of our homes at this time of year—or, at least, we should. We should use this time of chilly weather to slow down, relax, and reconnect with ourselves. Only then will we have anything to offer our families and friends, our bosses and co-workers.

Awaken your heart. Get out of the busy, mind-numbing trance of contemporary life. Interrupt your day-to-day pattern and celebrate taking a break. Decide to embrace slowness.

Listen to the wind. Sit and feel the sun on your skin. Sing out loud and look at the world. Listen to the words within you and write them down.

Be still. Celebrate a slower pace.

Celebrate a Pause

Be still and know that I am God.
— The Bible

Celebrate a Pause

Deafened by the voice of desire, you are unaware the
Beloved lives in the core of your heart. Stop the noise
and you will hear His voice in the silence.
— Rumi

Celebrate a Pause

There is a quality to being alone that is incredibly precious.
Life rushes back to the void, richer, more vivid, fuller than before.
– Anne Morrow Lindbergh

Celebrate a Pause

Every now and then go away, have a little relaxation, for when you come back to your work, your judgment will be surer.
— Leonardo DaVinci

Celebrate a Pause

In the solitude of your mind are the answers to all your questions about life. You must take the time to ask and listen.
– Mahaiyaddeen

Celebrate a Pause

Take rest; a field that has rested gives a bountiful crop.
– Ovid

Celebrate a Pause

We spend most of our time and energy in a kind of horizontal thinking. We move along the surface of things...[but] there are times when we stop. We sit still. We lose ourselves in a pile of leaves or its memory. We listen and breezes from a whole other world begin to whisper.
– James Carroll

Celebrate a Pause

Solitude is the place of purification.
— Martin Buber

Celebrate a Pause

You must learn to be still in the midst of activity
and to be vibrantly alive in repose.
– Indira Gandhi

Celebrate a Pause

Calmness is the cradle of power.
— Josiah Gilbert Holland

NOVEMBER

Celebrate Your Sisters

November

Celebrate Your Sisters

We women are more alike than different. Therefore we can embrace the women in our lives, even if we are not automatically drawn to this or that personality. Women nurture, heal, comfort, guide, mother, mentor and teach – this is our nature. As women, we are sisters, and the benefits we reap from one another can be extraordinary.

I remember my adopted sister, who was five years older than me. In the small room we shared, my sister shoved her bed between our bedroom door and my bed. She made herself a barrier against the abuse of my stepfather. By becoming a wall, she buffered the violence and protected me. This is what sisters can do for one another. We can protect each other, we can look out for one another. We can offer a wall of security. We can take away darkness from each other so one's light can shine.

November is a month that we express gratitude, a month of Thanksgiving, family, ceremony, and celebration.

Take time this month to celebrate your sisters. Embrace the women in your life who absorb the darkness and allow you to shine. Be a sister for another.

Celebrate Your Sisters

We don't accomplish anything in this world alone ... and whatever happens is the result of the whole tapestry of one's life and all the weavings of individual threads from one to another that create something.
– Sandra Day O'Connor

Celebrate Your Sisters

Friendship is…the sort of love one can imagine between angels.
– C. S. Lewis

Celebrate Your Sisters

Help us to be the always hopeful gardeners of the spirit
who know that without darkness nothing comes to birth,
as without light nothing flowers.
— May Sarton

Celebrate Your Sisters

Whenever you see darkness, there is extraordinary opportunity for the light to burn brighter.

– Bono

Celebrate Your Sisters

Our belief in one another is what unites us
and encourages us to be our best.
– Sarah McLachlan

Celebrate Your Sisters

At times our own light goes out and is rekindled by a spark from another person. Each of us has cause to think with deep gratitude of those who have lighted the flame within us.
– Albert Schweitzer

Celebrate Your Sisters

We are all travelers in the wilderness of this world and the best that we find is an honest friend. He is a fortunate voyager who finds many. They are the end and reward of life.
– Robert Louis Stevenson

Celebrate Your Sisters

Forget injuries, never forget kindness.
– Confucius

Celebrate Your Sisters

Do a deed of simple kindness; Though its end you may not see,
It may reach, like widening ripples, down a long eternity.
– Joseph Norris

Celebrate Your Sisters

How important it is for us to recognize and celebrate
our heroes and she-roes!
– Maya Angelou

DECEMBER

Celebrate the Life You are NOT Living

December

Celebrate the Life You are NOT Living

On your journey, there have been many forks in the road. You had options, paths you could have chosen but did not. Should you have gone right or taken a left turn? This question presented itself many times as you walked your road of life.

We must make peace with the life we decided not to live, the life that could have been. Every step has served a greater purpose, even if we don't always see this purpose. We must trust in the certainty that we are living the life we were designed to live. We are becoming the beings we were destined to be. Especially when we resolve to listen to our hearts, we grow more aware of who it is we want to be. While accepting the "missteps" of the past, we go forward, secure in ourselves.

It may feel as though you have chosen the longest route possible to accomplish this journey of yours, your special mission. But you have taken the turns necessary for the lessons you needed to learn – and the lessons you provided for others.

As the year comes to a close, let go of your limiting "if-only" beliefs. Resolve never to think that you should have done this or that. Instead, embrace the life you have chosen and stay awake to the possibilities of tomorrow.

Celebrate the Life You are NOT Living

Life is a wondrous phenomenon.
— Albert Szent-Gyorgyi

Celebrate the Life You are NOT Living

"...you are actually connected to all that you desire to manifest, and you know this to be your truth."
— Wayne Dyer

Celebrate the Life You are NOT Living

"Take the first step in faith. You don't have to see the whole staircase, just take the first step."
– Martin Luther King, Jr.

Celebrate the Life You are NOT Living

"Some people think it's holding on that makes one strong;
sometimes it's letting go."
– Sylvia Robinson

Celebrate the Life You are NOT Living

"It is a mistake to try to look too far ahead. The chain of destiny can only be grasped one link at a time."
— Sir Winston Churchill

Celebrate the Life You are NOT Living

Your best teacher is your last mistake.
— Ralph Nader

Celebrate the Life You are NOT Living

Letting go is like releasing a tight spring at the core of yourself,
one you've spent your whole life winding and maintaining.
When you let go, you grow still and quiet.
— Sue Monk Kidd

Celebrate the Life You are NOT Living

There is an important difference between giving up and letting go.
— Jessica Hatchigan

Celebrate the Life You are NOT Living

Success is to be measured not so much by the position that one has achieved in life as by the obstacles which he has overcome.
— Booker T. Washington

Celebrate the Life You are NOT Living

Throughout the centuries there were men who took first steps, down new roads, armed with nothing but their own vision.
– Ayn Rand

Order Form

Item	Price	Qty	Subtotal
The Art of Self Discovery	$19.95	___	_____
The Inner Fitness for Empowerment Journal	$14.95	___	_____
The Inner Fitness for Girls Journal	$14.95	___	_____
The Inner Fitness for Celebrating Your Life Journal	$14.95	___	_____

SUBTOTAL: (please add $2 per item for Shipping & Handling) _____

TOTAL: _____

MC, Visa, Discover and Am Ex accepted

__ MC   __ Visa   __ Discover   __ Am Ex

Acct No._____   Exp. Date_____

Signature_____
(Credit card charges will appear as InsideOut Publishing)

Name_____
Address_____
Phone_____ E-mail_____

OR check or money order (made payable to address below).

Send orders to:
InsideOut Publishing • PO Box 1477 • Eagle, ID 83616

InsideOut Publishing • 208-794-5578 • www.inner-element.com

NutriMin C®
RE⁹

Celebrate Your Beauty!
with
ARBONNE®
INTERNATIONAL

Contact Jan Wheatley, Independent Consultant, for a **FREE** Color Consultation today:
jan@jwheatley.com or (208) 887-1139

THESE MATERIALS HAVE BEEN PRODUCED BY JAN WHEATLEY, AN ARBONNE INDEPENDENT CONSULTANT, AND ARE NOT OFFICIAL MATERIALS PREPARED OR PROVIDED BY ARBONNE INTERNATIONAL, LLC. ARBONNE MAKES NO PROMISES OR GUARANTEES THAT ANY CONSULTANT WILL BE FINANCIALLY SUCCESSFUL AS EACH CONSULTANT'S RESULTS ARE DEPENDENT ON HIS OR HER OWN SKILL AND EFFORT.

The market fluctuates, my standards don't

Suzi Boyle
Mortgage Originator

Trusted by Idaho, Recognized Nationally

"Celebrating Women Celebrating Life"

EVERGREEN HOME LOANS

Toll Free: 1-888-821-9233
Telephone: 208-327-5586
Suzi Direct: 208-344-4719
suziboyle@evergreenhomeloans.com
Check out my website -
www.suziboyle.com

EQUAL OPPORTUNITY LENDER

Notes…

Notes…